DATE DUE			

The Civil War

Library of Congress Cataloging-in-Publication Data

The Civil War
     (Wars that changed the world; v. 2)
     Includes index.
     Summary: A history of one of the great wars that
changed the course of events in America, the Civil
War.
     1. United States—History—Civil War, l861-1865—Juvenile literature. [1.
United States—History—
Civil War, l861-1865] I. Marshall Cavendish Corporation
II. Series.
E468.A5 l988   973.7   88-2855
ISBN 0-86307-929-6 (set)
ISBN 0-86307-933-4 (v. 2)

Reference Edition Published l988

Published by Marshall Cavendish Corporation
147 West Merrick Road
Freeport, Long Island
N.Y. 11520

Printed in Italy by New Interlitho, Milan.

Designed and produced by
AS Publishing

WARS THAT CHANGED THE WORLD

The Civil War

By Philip Clark
Illustrated by Jack Keay and Richard Hook

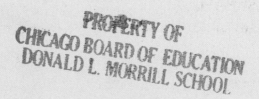
MARSHALL CAVENDISH
NEW YORK, LONDON, TORONTO

A House Divided

The American Civil War was the first major conflict to make full use of nineteenth-century technology. Troops were moved rapidly by rail; generals communicated with each other by telegraph; ironclads began to replace wooden ships. Trenches, barbed wire and even early machine-guns made their appearance on the battlefield. In many ways the Civil War foreshadowed the grim carnage of World War I.

The Growth of the United States

The original thirteen states were former British colonies on the Atlantic coast of North America. They had banded together to fight and defeat the British in the American

The United States on the eve of the Civil War. Nebraska and Kansas were part of a huge area bought from France in the 1803 Louisiana Purchase. Texas had won its independence from Mexico in 1836, and became a state in 1845. California and New Mexico were taken over after the Mexican War of 1848.

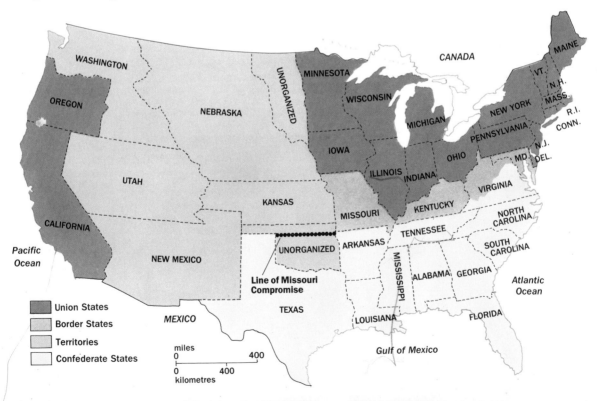

Line of Missouri Compromise

Union States
Border States
Territories
Confederate States

Revolution. But in the southern states particularly many people still believed that loyalty to their state was more important than loyalty to the Union.

The young country rapidly expanded by purchase and conquest until by the mid-1800s its borders had become much as they are today. However, the western lands were still thinly populated. As settlers poured in, new states were admitted to the Union. (A territory needed a population of at least 60,000 to apply for statehood.)

The Slavery Issue

The admittance of new states to the Union brought sharply into focus the problem of slavery. The cotton plantations of the South were worked largely by black slaves. Politicians clashed angrily on the question of whether the new states should or should not permit slavery.

The Missouri Compromise of 1821 had been an attempt to satisfy both parties. It stated that in the huge area then known as Louisiana (bought from France in 1803) slavery should be prohibited north of latitude 36°30′ North (except in Missouri itself).

The Kansas-Nebraska Bill of 1854 effectively put an end to the Missouri Compromise, which had been a kind of peace treaty between northern and southern states. It introduced the idea of new states making up their own minds on the slavery question.

One result was the formation of the Republican Party, which was dedicated to preventing the spread of slavery into new states. The southern slave states feared that they would be greatly outnumbered in the Congress by the free states. This encouraged them to form a Confederacy, an alliance that almost became a breakaway nation.

Frederick Douglass (1817-1895) was the best-known black campaigner against slavery. Himself born a slave, Douglass escaped and eventually fled abroad. (Under Federal law, free states had to return fugitive slaves to their owners.) Douglass returned and bought his freedom with money earned from lectures. During the war he urged the Union to make greater use of black troops.

The Dred Scott Case Dred Scott was a slave from Missouri who claimed his freedom because he had once been taken to a free state. In 1857, Chief Justice Roger Taney ruled that slaves were property, and as such could be taken anywhere in the United States. This incident, by enraging public opinion in the North, helped to bring the Civil War one step closer.

North and South

There is no simple answer to the question "What caused the Civil War?." The slavery issue is a large part of the reason, but it is not the whole answer. There was also the question of whether an individual state had the right to secede from (leave) the Union. And then there was the conflict between two very different ways of life, based on quite different attitudes and beliefs.

At the time of George Washington, the main southern crop had been tobacco. Black slaves were imported from Africa on a large scale to work on the plantations. But then the Industrial Revolution in Britain resulted in machines that could process cotton into clothing. Cotton took over from tobacco as the South's main crop, although during the War it was largely replaced by corn.

The North in the meantime had become increasingly industrialized, and as a result no longer needed slave labor. Its factories were also to play a major part in deciding the outcome of the war.

The Old Way

The southern states stuck to their traditional way of life, based on the cotton plantations with their slave labor and large white mansions. The leisured classes rode their horses, they played cards and danced, and they read the romantic novels of Sir Walter Scott. They wished to be left alone to live their lives in their own way.

Some families treated their slaves reasonably well, but in most cases slaves were forced to work from dawn to dusk under conditions of great hardship. Harriet Beecher Stowe's novel *Uncle Tom's Cabin* helped persuade Northerners of the evils of slavery.

A prosperous southern cotton plantation at harvest time. The scene looks peaceful enough, but the slaves had to work punishingly long hours under the blazing sun. During the Civil War, the Union blockade prevented the Confederate states from exporting more than a fraction of the crop.

Balance Sheet

The Union went into the war with formidable advantages. It had a population of some 22 million, while the South's nine million included about 3,500,000 slaves. The North was much richer and had far more factories. It proved more successful than the South in producing guns, uniforms, clothing and other military supplies. By virtue of its navy, it was able to squeeze the Confederacy with a powerful blockade. Finally, the North had a better rail network by which to move troops and supplies.

The South had far fewer areas of superiority. Many Southerners were good horsemen and fine shots. But the Confederacy's main asset was the quality of its military leaders, although even this advantage was blunted by the continual interference of President Jefferson Davis.

John Brown
John Brown was an anti-slavery fanatic who devised a plan to start a slave rebellion. In 1859 he led a small band to capture the Federal arsenal at Harpers Ferry in West Virginia. The attempt failed and Brown was later hanged. The detachment of marines that captured him was under the command of Colonel (later General) Robert E. Lee.

The Union Splits

On November 6th, 1860, Abraham Lincoln was elected the sixteenth President of the United States. He had joined the new Republican Party in 1856. Since the Republican Party was committed to banning slavery in new states and territories, the South had been waiting anxiously for the election result. On December 20th, South Carolina voted to secede from the Union, to be followed soon afterwards by six more states: Mississippi, Florida, Alabama, Georgia, Louisiana and Texas.

For Lincoln, preservation of the Union was a solemn duty. As an olive branch to the South, he offered to retain slavery in states where it was not already illegal. But he asserted that no state had the right to leave the Union.

The election of Abraham Lincoln as President of the United States made civil war almost inevitable, as he believed he had a duty to hold the Union together. Behind Lincoln is the 1861 33-star flag under which the Union armies fought the first half of the war. He refused to remove the stars of the southern states.

The War Begins

Lincoln made clear his determination to protect Federal (Union) property in the South. This included Fort Sumter, in Charleston Harbor, South Carolina. The government of South Carolina demanded that the fort be evacuated. Instead, the fort's commanding officer, Major Robert Anderson, prepared for its defense.

By neither evacuating nor reinforcing Fort Sumter, Lincoln made sure that the South would have to fire the first shot. The bombardment of the fort began on April 12th, 1861, and Anderson duly surrendered to representatives of the Confederate commander.

Lincoln's immediate reaction was to call for 75,000 volunteers to join the Union Army and to order a blockade of Confederate ports. Four more states – Virginia, Arkansas, North Carolina and Tennessee – joined the Confederacy.

The border states of Missouri, Kentucky, Maryland and Delaware remained in the Union, but the first two in particular contained a strong pro-Confederate faction. As always with civil wars, the conflict divided friends and families. It also strained the loyalties of U.S. Army officers whose states joined the Confederacy. Robert E. Lee was actually offered the command of the Union Army. But with great reluctance, he decided that loyalty to his state came first, and a few days later he accepted command of the Virginian forces. In the meantime the newly-formed Confederate States of America elected as their president Jefferson Davis, a former soldier.

The war began on April 12th, 1861, when Confederate batteries opened fire on Fort Sumter in Charleston Harbor, South Carolina. Two days later, the fort's garrison surrendered to Brigadier General P. G. T. Beauregard. Fort Sumter remained in Confederate hands until the very end of the war.

The Opening Battles

The first major battle of the war was fought at Bull Run near the Potomac River. (The two sides often had different names for the same battle. Bull Run was called Manassas by the Confederates.)

A Union army under Brigadier General Irwin McDowell attacked the Confederates on July 21st, 1861. At first, the Rebels were able to hold off the attacks. Then William T. Sherman's brigade broke through their line. As the Southerners fled, their general spotted the disciplined ranks of Brigadier General Thomas J. Jackson standing their ground. "There is Jackson standing like a stone wall. Rally behind the Virginians!" The name stuck and "Stonewall" Jackson he became. The line held.

Both sides were tiring, and the balance was finally tipped in the Confederates' favor by the arrival of Jubal Early's brigade. The Union troops retreated, and the retreat became a panic-stricken flight, involving civilians who had come out from Washington to watch the battle. The South had won, but the soldiers were too exhausted to follow up their victory and march on Washington. Lincoln replaced McDowell with Major General George B. McClellan.

During the remainder of 1861, both sides engaged in a struggle for Kentucky. Union control of the state was ensured by the capture of Forts Henry and Donelson by Brigadier General Ulysses S. Grant in February 1862.

Shiloh

Union strategy hardened into a campaign to secure control of the Mississippi River, and thus split the Confederacy. On the morning of April 6th, Grant was

The Confederacy chose Jefferson Davis as its president. Davis attempted to combine the roles of president and Commander-in-Chief. As a result, his continued interference in purely military matters, particularly his reluctance to fire incompetent generals, proved disastrous for the South.

encamped near Shiloh Church, Pittsburg Landing, Tennessee. There his army was taken almost completely by surprise by a Confederate army under Albert Sidney Johnston.

The battle was fought with deadly ferocity. By the end of the first day the Rebels had had the better of the contest, though Johnston was dead. The following day Grant counter-attacked, and the Confederates were eventually forced to retreat.

Over 100,000 soldiers fought at Shiloh and nearly a quarter of them were listed as killed, wounded or missing. Although Shiloh was a Union victory, Union losses were actually greater.

Chased by Confederate cavalry, Federal troops retreat across Bull Run Creek. Tired, hungry, and short of ammunition, the southern army made only a token pursuit of its beaten enemy. Even so, it was to be a long time before the North recovered from the humiliation of its defeat at Bull Run.

11

The Armies

At the outbreak of war, the United States had only a tiny professional army. This was in theory supported by the states' volunteer militias. It was not long, however, before the supply of volunteers proved inadequate, and both sides brought in the draft, or conscription – the South in 1862, the Union in the following year.

At first regiments paraded in a variety of uniforms, many of them more decorative than practical. At the First Battle of Bull Run, the two sides had considerable difficulty distinguishing friend from foe. As a result, uniforms became more standardized. The Union adopted the dark blue jackets of the United States Army while the Confederates chose "cadet gray." Northern soldiers were nicknamed Billy Yank, and Southerners Johnny Reb.

Clara Barton (1821-1912) the "Angel of the Battlefields," organized the nursing of wounded Union troops throughout the war. She also founded the American Red Cross.

A Union infantryman loads his single-shot Springfield rifle. This tedious process involved biting the end off a paper cartridge and pouring the powder down the rifle barrel. Then the bullet had to be rammed home. Finally the weapon would be primed by inserting a percussion cap underneath the hammer.

Weapons

In this area, as in most others, the Union soldier was better equipped than his Southern counterpart.

There was a steady improvement in the quality of firearms as the war went on. Smoothbore muskets were gradually replaced by the more accurate rifle musket, in which a spiral groove in the barrel spun the bullet in flight to achieve greater accuracy and range. Cavalry favored the shorter carbine. The single-shot Sharps Carbine was later superceded by the Spencer Carbine, which held eight shots.

The Civil War also saw a progressive transition from smoothbore to rifled field guns, such as the Parrot and Rodman models.

Gunners as well as officers wore swords, but both sides came to prefer pistols for close fighting. Again, single-shot smoothbore pistols were replaced by revolvers with rifled barrels.

Because of the increasing accuracy and sophistication of firearms, casualties were extremely heavy. And yet time and again soldiers from both sides would go on fighting while men were shot down all around them. Battlefields were fearful places, littered with corpses, and wounded men and horses in every stage of agony and mutilation.

Even for those wounded who were fortunate enough to get to a hospital, the chances of death from infected wounds or disease were high. In the early stages of the war, both sides exchanged prisoners at suitable opportunities. Later on, these arrangements broke down. Towards the end of the war, the South had great difficulty in feeding its own people, let alone its prisoners. Conditions in some of the South's prison camps, notably Andersonville, Georgia, were appalling.

Confederate artillerymen prepare to fire a Parrot field gun.

The War at Sea

Mines and Torpedoes
In August 1864, Admiral Farragut attacked the Confederate fleet in Mobile Bay. The defenders used "moored torpedoes" (mines) to protect the bay's approaches. At the height of the battle, Farragut is supposed to have shouted "Damn the torpedoes! Full speed ahead!"

In October of the same year, 21-year-old Lieutenant William B. Cushing used a torpedo fixed to a pole in the bows of a small boat to sink the Confederate ironclad *Albemarle*.

The historic, though inconclusive duel between the *Monitor* (foreground) and the *Merrimac*. Although both Britain and France had built armoured ships before the Civil War, this was the first battle between two ironclads. Afterwards, both sides realized that the days of the wooden-hulled warship were numbered, and both set to work to construct new and better ironclads.

When Lincoln ordered a blockade of Southern ports, the Union had a total of about 90 ships. However, less than half were ready for sea, and many more were out-of-date sailing vessels. The Confederacy had almost no navy at all, although it did have plenty of experienced naval officers. It had to buy ships from abroad and from private owners to act as blockade runners and commerce raiders. Even so, it soon built up a respectable fleet.

The North made use of armed merchant vessels to enforce its blockade. The South lost one major port after another. In April 1862 Admiral David G. Farragut destroyed a Confederate fleet at New Orleans at the mouth of the Mississippi, and went on to take the city. In August 1864 Farragut closed one of the last remaining Confederate ports when he won the Battle of Mobile Bay, although the city of Mobile itself held out until the end of the war.

The Battle of the Ironclads

Both sides experimented with armor-plated warships. The Confederates salvaged a Union steam freighter called the *Merrimac*, and rebuilt it as an ironclad. The Union retaliated by building an even odder-looking ironclad, called the *Monitor*.

On March 8th, 1862 the *Merrimac* steamed out of Norfolk, Virginia, into Hampton Roads. She destroyed two Union ships and three more ran aground attempting to protect them. The next day the *Monitor* gave battle. The two ironclads fired away at each other but neither's guns were able to penetrate the other's armor-plating and the battle ended in stalemate.

The War in the East

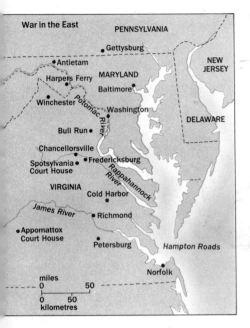

The Confederates had hoped to use the *Merrimac* to help block McClellan's advance on Richmond. However, when they abandoned Norfolk, Virginia, in May 1862, the Confederates burned and scuttled her. The ironclad drew too much water to sail up the James River to Richmond, and she was too unseaworthy to move to another Confederate port.

George B. McClellan was made General-in-Chief of the Union armies in December 1861. Prodded by Lincoln, he began his advance on Richmond, the Confederate capital. He moved his army by sea to the Virginia Peninsula, south-east of the city, and promptly got locked into a siege at Yorktown. This gave the Confederates ample time to fortify the approaches to their capital. (At this stage of the war, the North relied for intelligence gathering on Allan Pinkerton's famous detective agency, which damaged the Union war effort by grossly overestimating enemy numbers.)

It was not until May 1862 that McClellan got close to Richmond. A badly organized Confederate attack at Fair Oaks (Seven Pines) was beaten back, and General Joseph E. Johnston, the Southern commander, was severely wounded. This apparent set-back actually benefited the South, for President Davis replaced Johnston with Robert E. Lee.

The Valley Campaign

Part of the Union army had stayed to defend Washington. The Confederates were anxious to prevent these troops from reinforcing McClellan. Lee, at that time serving as Davis's military adviser, had suggested to Stonewall Jackson that he should create a diversion in the Shenandoah Valley.

Jackson's campaign was brilliant. With no more than 17,000 men, he tied down much larger Union armies, on which he inflicted heavy casualties. His men covered ground so rapidly that they became known as the "foot cavalry." Jackson rejoined Lee's army in late June.

The Seven Days' Battles

Lee was the archetype of the reserved and courteous Southern gentleman. He was also a great general. Even Jackson, no particular respecter of persons, said of Lee, "He is the only man I would follow blindfold."

Lee now sent Jeb Stuart's cavalry to report on McClellan's troop positions. In a daring raid, the dashing Stuart and his troopers rode right around the Northern Army of the Potomac. On June 25th, Lee, now reinforced by Jackson, launched the first of a series of attacks on McClellan's army. These were repulsed by the Union troops, but McClellan finally retreated. Lee had removed the threat to Richmond, but he had suffered heavy losses in the process.

Second Bull Run

Lincoln now formed a new army based on the troops defending Washington, and put Major General John Pope in command. McClellan was ordered to join forces with Pope. With the threat to Richmond removed, Lee decided to attack Pope before McClellan could link up with him. The result was the Second Battle of Bull Run (Second Manassas) where on August 29th-30th Pope was soundly beaten by a smaller Confederate army under Lee and Jackson. The remains of Pope's forces were absorbed into McClellan's Army of the Potomac.

Lee Invades the North

Lee now decided to carry the war into enemy territory, in the hope of gaining foreign recognition and military aid. An invasion of Maryland would also reduce the pressure on Southern supplies. Throughout the war, the South had difficulty keeping its troops adequately fed and clothed.

General George B. McClellan ("Little Mac") was a brilliant organizer, and turned the dispirited Army of the Potomac into a fighting force to be reckoned with. His main fault was his excessive caution, caused chiefly by his reluctance to sacrifice the lives of his men. Despite this, Lee said after the war that McClellan was the only Union general who kept him awake at night.

Antietam

McClellan had a remarkable stroke of luck when, on September 13th, a Union soldier found a copy of Lee's orders in an envelope wrapped around some cigars. Typically McClellan moved just too slowly to capitalize fully on this find. Lee had dangerously divided his force by sending Jackson to capture Harpers Ferry. However, Jackson managed to rejoin Lee before McClellan struck. Instead of retreating in the face of superior numbers, Lee chose to stand and fight at Antietam Creek (Sharpsburg) on the Potomac River.

On September 17th, McClellan launched his attack. In the fierce fighting that followed, the two armies battered each other to a standstill. Casualties were alarmingly heavy, both sides having around 12,000 soldiers killed or wounded. Lee remained in his position the following day, but his invasion was over. He had no choice left except to retreat across the Potomac.

Fredericksburg and Chancellorsville

McClellan failed to pursue Lee's army, and Lincoln finally lost patience with his General-in-Chief ("He has got the slows. . . ."). Lincoln replaced McClellan with General Burnside. On December 13th, 1862 Burnside launched a frontal attack on a strong Confederate position at Fredericksburg. Lee beat back the Army of the Potomac with heavy losses. Burnside resigned, and Lincoln tried yet another commander. This time he chose "Fighting Joe" Hooker. Hooker devised a plan to attack Lee's lines at Fredericksburg from the rear.

Lee, however, was too wily to fall into Hooker's trap. Learning from Jeb Stuart that the enemy were at Chancellorsville, Lee and Jackson marched to meet him,

General Ambrose E. Burnside
If Lee was the greatest commander of the war on either side, Burnside was probably the most inept. Well aware of his own shortcomings, "Burn" tried without success to refuse Lincoln's offer of command of the Army of the Potomac. After the disaster of Fredericksburg, Burnside was replaced at his own request. He was finally dismissed towards the end of the war for, as Lincoln is supposed to have said, "wringing one last spectacular defeat from the jaws of victory at the Battle of the Crater."

Burnside's splendid set of mutton-chop whiskers have given us the word "sideburns."

The Emancipation Proclamation
Lee's withdrawal after Antietam gave the Union the opportunity to declare the battle a Northern victory. On September 22nd, Lincoln issued his Preliminary Emancipation Proclamation. This stated that slaves in rebel territory were free, even though in practice many slaves had to await the end of the war to gain their freedom.

On May 2nd, 1863, Stonewall Jackson rode out beyond his own lines at Chancellorsville, looking for a way of cutting off the Federal retreat. On his return, he was accidentally shot by his own troops. He died a week later. Lee believed that he would have won the Battle of Gettysburg if Jackson had been there.

through a heavily wooded area known as the Wilderness.

Jackson reached Hooker's position in the evening of May 2nd, 1863 and attacked immediately. Hooker had already dug in, but as the Confederate attack developed he appeared to lose his nerve. Three days later he ordered a retreat.

It was another victory for Lee. But Jackson had been accidentally wounded by his own men. He died a week later, murmuring in delirium, "Let us cross over the river and rest under the shade of the trees." Lee was devastated: Jackson's death was an irreparable disaster for the Confederacy.

Confederate High Tide

In the West, Grant was attempting to gain full control of the Mississippi by taking the key Confederate stronghold of Vicksburg. He spent the early months of 1863 trying out various schemes, including an attempt to bypass the city by cutting a canal, but all were failures. However, in April, a Union flotilla managed to slip past the Confederate defenses by night. Grant, who had cut loose from his supply lines and determined to live off the countryside, settled down for a siege.

Gettysburg

On June 3rd, Lee's army began another invasion of the North. Lee hoped that this might draw Grant's forces away from Vicksburg. But things started to go wrong when Stuart went off on one of his cavalry raids, and left the army without its "eyes" for ten critical days.

The army moved forward, in the words of one of Lee's officers, "Like a blindfolded giant." One division marched towards the small town of Gettysburg, Pennsylvania, having heard a rumor that the Union depot there contained a supply of much-needed shoes. On July 1st they encountered a division of Union cavalry, and managed to outmaneuver them. As the Confederates forced the Northerners back, Lee decided to fight a major battle.

Pushed out of the town, the Union front-line troops, under General George G. Meade, occupied strong positions on Culp's Hill and Cemetery Hill. The next day saw gallant but poorly coordinated Confederate attacks which narrowly failed to take the Union positions. On the third day, after a tremendous artillery duel, Lee decided on a last stab – a frontal attack upon Cemetery Ridge.

Pickett's Charge – the Confederates reach Cemetery Ridge. General Armistead holds his hat on his sword to indicate the direction of the attack. Fierce hand-to-hand fighting followed, in which Armistead was mortally wounded. Finally, Union reinforcements drove the Confederates from the ridge.

Pickett's Charge

The attack was made by the newly-arrived troops of Major General George E. Pickett. Pickett's 15,000 men marched into a hail of fire and into history. Less than a thousand reached their objective – too few to hold it. Some of the tiny remnants of the attack surrendered, others retreated to their own lines. Lee had gambled and lost. Characteristically, he took the responsibility. "It was all my fault this time. . . .".

Lee's only option after the battle was to retreat. He managed to get the remains of his battered army back across the Potomac. Meade made little attempt to stop him. Casualties were the worst of the war so far. Meade had lost a quarter of his army; Lee over a third.

On July 4th, the day Lee began his retreat to Virginia, the defenders of Vicksburg surrendered to General Grant.

The capture of Vicksburg gave the North complete control of the Mississippi, splitting the South in two.

The River of Death

If Vicksburg was the key to control of the Mississippi, the strategic centre of Southern rail communications was the city of Chattanooga, Tennessee. In the summer of 1863, Chattanooga was defended by the Confederate Army of Tennessee under General Braxton Bragg.

Under pressure from the Union Army of the Cumberland under William S. Rosecrans, Bragg evacuated Chattanooga on September 6th and retreated into Geor-

The "Battle Above the Clouds." Union troops under General Hooker assault the Confederate position on Lookout Mountain. The defenders put up a spirited resistance, but were forced back by superior numbers.

gia. Rosecrans pursued him, unaware that Bragg was awaiting reinforcements in the shape of James Longstreet's corps from Lee's Army of Northern Virginia. Both armies concentrated their forces near Chickamauga (a Cherokee Indian word meaning "River of Death").

The Battle of Chickamauga

Fighting began in earnest on September 19th. Neither side had gained the advantage when Longstreet arrived later that day. When fighting resumed the following morning, Longstreet found himself facing a gap in the Union right wing. Giving the famous "Rebel yell", his men stormed through it. The Union right flank broke. Only the Union left was held, under Major General George H. Thomas, whose steady performance was to earn him the nickname of "the Rock of Chickamauga."

The Army of the Cumberland withdrew to Chattanooga, while the Confederates established themselves in strong positions on the high ground above the town.

The Battle of Chattanooga

On October 23rd, Grant arrived in Chattanooga, having been appointed Commander-in-Chief in the West. He immediately replaced Rosecrans with Thomas, brought in reinforcements, and reorganized the Union supply lines.

In November Grant launched his army against Bragg's positions on Lookout Mountain and Missionary Ridge. The Confederates were beaten back by overwhelming numbers. Grant had achieved the North's objective of taking Chattanooga, and gained control of the state of Tennessee. Having split the Confederacy from north to south along the Mississippi, Union forces were now in a position to split it once more, this time from west to east.

Grant Versus Lee

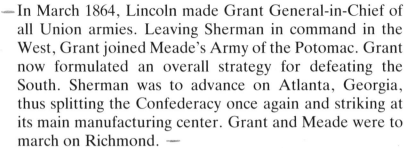

In March 1864, Lincoln made Grant General-in-Chief of all Union armies. Leaving Sherman in command in the West, Grant joined Meade's Army of the Potomac. Grant now formulated an overall strategy for defeating the South. Sherman was to advance on Atlanta, Georgia, thus splitting the Confederacy once again and striking at its main manufacturing center. Grant and Meade were to march on Richmond.

Contemporaries agree that General Grant's appearance was unimpressive. He had been a failure in civilian life and was rumored to have a drinking problem. Yet he became the best Union general of the war.

The Battle of the Wilderness

Grant's route to Richmond took his army once again through the tangled woods of the Wilderness. Lee marched his troops up to stop him. The battle began on May 5th and lasted for two days. The fighting was fiercer than ever, and casualties were heavy. Grant's losses were greater, but he had more men to lose.

There were grim reminders of Chancellorsville. Many of the wounded were burned to death when the underbrush caught fire. And Longstreet was seriously wounded by his own side near where Jackson had been shot the previous year. On May 11th the gallant Jeb Stuart was killed. Lee had now lost several of his ablest generals.

Grant refused to be diverted from his goal. He moved his army around Lee's left and advanced on Spotsylvania Court House. Lee had anticipated Grant's move and his troops rapidly constructed defensive lines of trenches protected by log breastworks. On May 12th Grant attacked a bulge in the Confederate line called the Mule Shoe. The western part of the bulge became known as Bloody Angle from the incredible ferocity of the fighting. But again the Confederate line held.

Cold Harbor

The final battle in this phase of Grant's drive on Richmond took place at Cold Harbor. On June 3rd, Grant launched a massive frontal attack on Lee's entrenchments. It was beaten back with huge losses.

By this time Grant's campaign had cost the North over 50,000 casualties. Lee's losses were always fewer. But Grant had grasped the essential fact that he could replace his dead and wounded much more easily than Lee could. He was determined to go on grinding his enemy down until "there should be nothing left of him."

The Union Closes In

During the stiflingly hot summer days of 1864, Grant was forced to change his tactics. Lee had skillfully headed him off from a direct assault on Richmond. And public opinion in the North was finding Grant's "butcher's bill" unacceptably high.

Grant decided to strike south to Petersburg, a rail center through which Richmond's supplies passed. If Grant could take Petersburg, Richmond could no longer be defended. In the middle of June, Grant moved his army across the James River on an enormously long pontoon bridge.

Petersburg was defended by a small force under General Beauregard. A rapid and well-coordinated Union attack might have taken the city. But the piecemeal Union attacks were bungled. Lee was able to reinforce Beauregard, and Grant was forced to settle for a siege.

On July 30th, Union mining engineers blew a huge gap in the Confederate defences. But the Northern (mainly black) attackers were cut to pieces in the Battle of the Crater.

General Robert E. Lee was belatedly appointed Commander-in-Chief of all Confederate forces on February 6th, 1865. By this time, the move was far too late to influence the outcome of the war.

Sherman's March

While Grant and Lee were still slugging it out, Sherman marched his army out from its base at Chattanooga towards Atlanta. Joseph E. Johnston conducted a masterly defense with his smaller Confederate force, and repulsed most of Sherman's attacks.

However, President Davis was dissatisfied with Johnston's defensive tactics, and replaced him with General John B. Hood. Hood went on to the attack, but was beaten back with heavy losses. He then retreated behind the defenses of Atlanta, surrounded by Sherman's army. Further Confederate attacks failed, and by the end of August, Sherman had cut the rail communications with the city. Hood evacuated Atlanta on September 1st. The following day the city was occupied by Union forces.

From Atlanta to the Sea

Hood retraced his steps in a desperate bid to sever Sherman's rail links with his base at Chattanooga. Leaving Thomas's army to deal with Hood, Sherman set off on his famous "March to the Sea." Determined to "make Georgia howl," Sherman advanced on a broad front, leaving a swath of destruction in his wake.

Hood still deluded himself that he could draw Sherman after him by invading Tennessee. Hood squandered his troops in fruitless attacks on Union positions, and his army was finally wrecked by Thomas in the Battle of Nashville in mid-December.

The coastal city of Savannah, Georgia, fell to Sherman on December 21st. He then continued his trail of destruction northward through the Carolinas, with the ultimate aim of linking up with Grant in Virginia.

William T. Sherman (above). His idea of war was to wage it on an entire nation (right). His March to the Sea (below) once again split the Confederacy, this time from west to east.

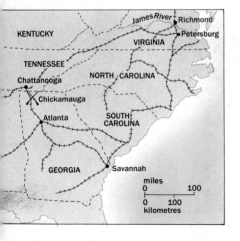

KENTUCKY

James River — Richmond
Petersburg
VIRGINIA

TENNESSEE
Chattanooga
NORTH CAROLINA
Chickamauga
Atlanta
SOUTH CAROLINA
GEORGIA — Savannah

miles
0   100
0   100
kilometres

The South is Defeated

Various peace feelers and a peace conference, had come to nothing, so Lee's only remaining course of action was to abandon Richmond and Petersburg. He hoped to link up with Johnston and defeat Sherman before Sherman could join forces with Grant. However, a Confederate attempt to break out of Petersburg on March 25th, was a failure. On April 2nd, Grant launched a massive attack on the city. During the heroic but doomed Confederate defense, A. P. Hill, one of the few remaining Southern generals of real ability, was killed.

Grant (left) shakes hands with Lee after the two generals had signed the surrender document. Lee had donned his full-dress uniform in anticipation of the event. Grant, who had come straight from the battlefield, apologized for his unkempt appearance (which he was always afterwards to regret).

The Army of Northern Virginia retreated westward. Lee hoped his troops would be able to join Johnston by rail, but Sheridan's cavalry arrived there first. Lee finally found the remains of his army surrounded. "Then there is nothing left me but to go and see General Grant," said Lee, "and I would rather die a thousand deaths."

Surrender at Appomattox

On Sunday April 9th, 1865, the two generals met at Appomattox Court House, Virginia. Grant was generous with his surrender terms (for which he was later critized). Lee pointed out that his soldiers owned their horses (which would be needed for the spring plowing) and Grant agreed that they could keep them. Finally, Grant's offer to supply Lee's men with rations was gratefully accepted. The two generals shook hands. Lee mounted his horse Traveler, and rode to bid his troops farewell.

As Commander-in-Chief, Lee could in theory have surrendered on behalf of all the Confederate armies. However, he still thought of himself as commanding officer of the Army of Northern Virginia. Johnston surrendered to Sherman on April 26th, 1865. The last Confederate army in the field surrendered on May 4th. Jefferson Davis was captured in Georgia, and was to spend two years imprisoned in Fort Monroe, Virginia.

Lincoln is Assassinated

On Good Friday, April 14th, Lincoln and his wife went to Ford's Theatre in Washington. While watching the play, Lincoln was shot by a Southern sympathizer named John Wilkes Booth. Lincoln died the following morning without recovering consciousness. Booth was hunted down and shot, and three of his fellow conspirators were hanged.

A Lasting Peace
With malice toward none; with charity for all; with firmness in the right, as God gives us to see the right, let us strive on the finish of the work we are in; to bind up the nation's wounds; to care for him who shall have borne the battle, and for his widow and his orphan – to do all which may achieve and cherish a just, and a lasting peace, among ourselves, and with all nations.
From Lincoln's second inaugural speech, March 4th, 1865.

Recollect that we form one country now. Abandon all local hatreds and make your sons Americans.
Robert E. Lee

From Lincoln's Gettysburg Address
'. . . we here highly resolve that these dead shall not have died in vain – that this nation, under God, shall have a new birth of freedom – and that government of the people, by the people, for the people, shall not perish from the earth.'
19 November 1863

The Aftermath

Over 600,000 men died in the Civil War. Of these, about 200,000 were killed in battle: the remaining two-thirds died of wounds or disease. The South lay in ruins. Lincoln's death was a tragedy for the South. He had seen his task as to "bind up the nation's wounds."

Some extreme members of the Republican Party wished to turn the South into a group of Republican states. They achieved their aim temporarily with the help of "carpetbaggers" (Northern political adventurers who manipulated the black vote).

However, slavery was dead, outlawed by the Thirteenth Amendment to the Constitution. The Fourteenth Amendment gave the freed slaves civil rights. But racial discrimination continued and another century would pass before black Americans achieved equal rights under the law.

The ruins of Richmond. The Confederate government abandoned their capital on April 2nd, 1865. They set fire to warehouses and military stores, the flames spread, and much of the city was destroyed. Richmond was occupied by Union troops the following day, and visited by Lincoln himself on April 4th.

Events of the War

1861

March 4th Lincoln inaugurated as President
April 12th Confederates attack Fort Sumter
July 21st First Battle of Bull Run (First Manassas)

1862

Feb 6th Grant captures Fort Henry on Tennessee River
Feb 16th Grant captures Fort Donelson
March 9th Naval battle between *Monitor* and *Merrimac*
April 6th-7th Battle of Shiloh
April 25th Admiral Farragut captures New Orleans
May 4th-June 9th Jackson's Shenandoah Valley Campaign
May 31st-June 1st Battle of Fair Oaks (Seven Pines)
June 25th-July 1st Seven Days' Battles
Aug 29-30 Second Battle of Bull Run (Second Manassas)
Sept 17th Battle of Antietam (Sharpsburg)
Sept 22nd Lincoln issues preliminary Emancipation Proclamation
Dec 13th Battle of Fredericksburg

1863

Jan 1st Lincoln issues Emancipation Proclamation
May 1st-4th Battle of Chancellorsville
April 16th-17th Admiral Porter takes Union flotilla past Vicksburg
July 1st-3rd Battle of Gettysburg
July 4th Grant takes Vicksburg
Sept 19th-20th Battle of Chickamauga

Nov 19th Lincoln delivers Gettysburg Address
Nov 23rd-25th Battle of Chattanooga

1864

March 9th Grant becomes General-in-Chief of Union armies
May 5th-6th Battle of the Wilderness
May 8th-12th Battle of Spotsylvania Court House
June 3rd Battle of Cold Harbor
June 20th Grant besieges Petersburg
July 11th-12th Confederate raid under Jubal Early almost reaches Washington
July 30th Battle of the Crater, Petersburg
Aug 5th Naval battle of Mobile Bay
Sept 2nd Sherman occupies Atlanta
Nov 6th Lincoln re-elected President
Nov 15th Sherman begins his March to the Sea
Dec 15th-16th Battle of Nashville
Dec 21st Sherman occupies Savannah

1865

Feb 6th Lee becomes General-in-Chief of Confederate armies
March 25th Confederate attempt to break out of Petersburg fails
April 2nd Confederates abandon Petersburg and Richmond
April 9th Lee surrenders to Grant at Appomattox Court House
April 14th Lincoln assassinated by John Wilkes Booth, and dies next day
April 26th Johnston surrenders to Sherman; John Wilkes Booth shot
May 4th Last Confederate army surrenders
May 26th Last Confederate troops surrender

Index